NOTRE DAME FIGHTING IRISH

BY
RAMEY TEMPLE

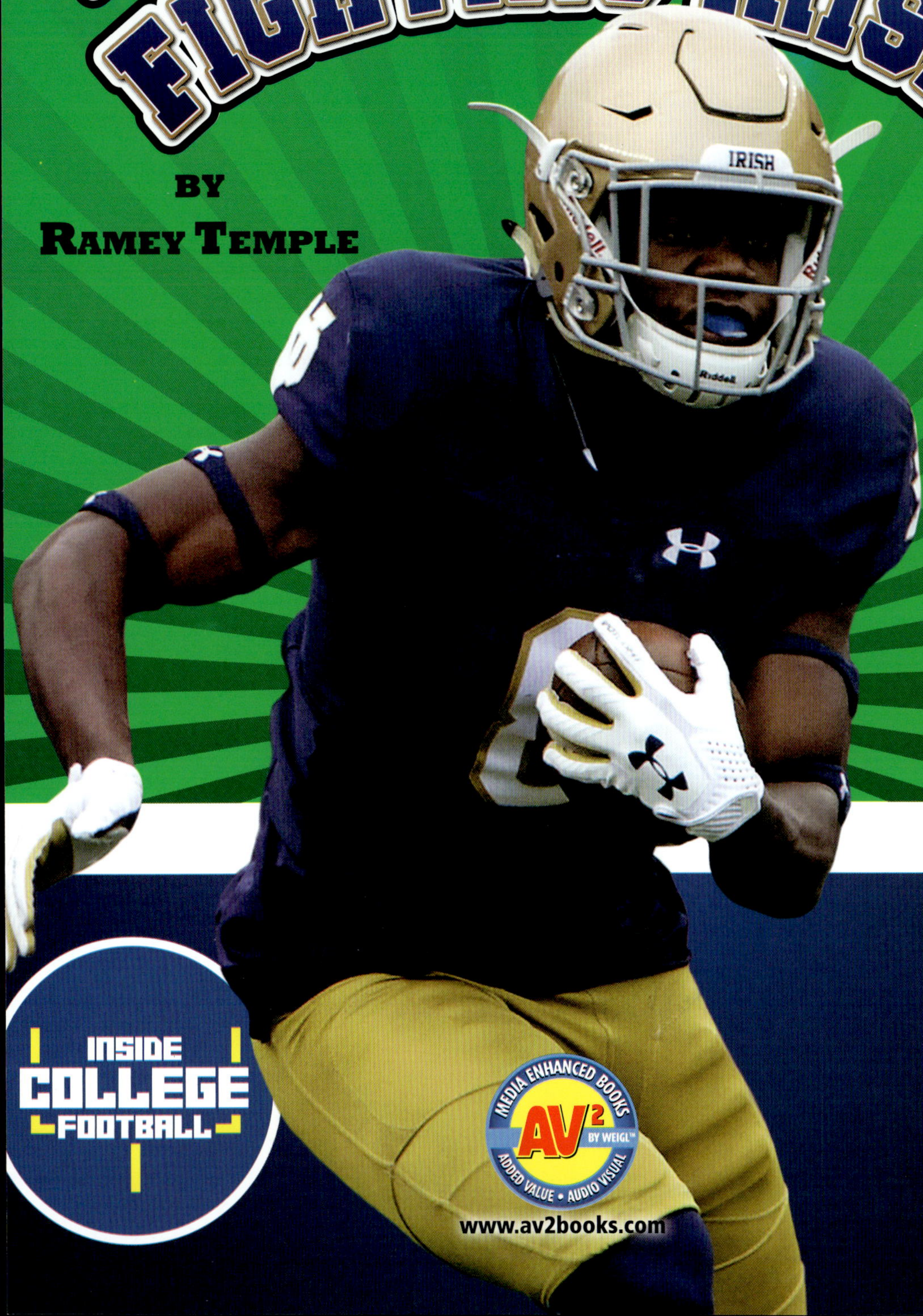

INSIDE COLLEGE FOOTBALL

MEDIA ENHANCED BOOKS
AV2 BY WEIGL
ADDED VALUE • AUDIO VISUAL
www.av2books.com

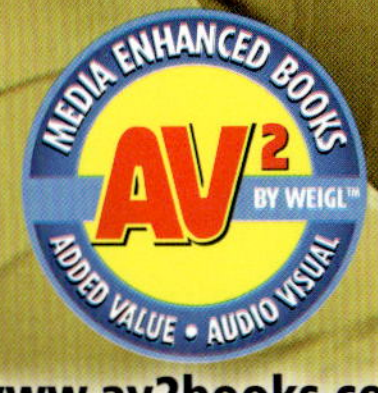

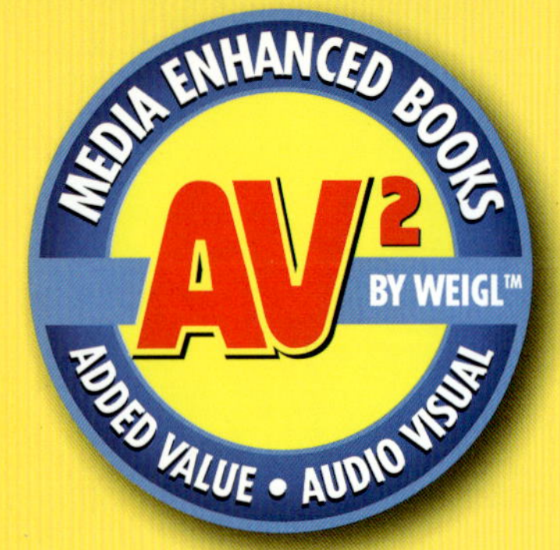

Go to www.av2books.com, and enter this book's unique code.

BOOK CODE

AVB63322

AV² by Weigl brings you media enhanced books that support active learning.

AV² provides enriched content that supplements and complements this book. Weigl's AV² books strive to create inspired learning and engage young minds in a total learning experience.

Your AV² Media Enhanced books come alive with...

Audio
Listen to sections of the book read aloud.

Key Words
Study vocabulary, and complete a matching word activity.

Video
Watch informative video clips.

Quizzes
Test your knowledge.

Embedded Weblinks
Gain additional information for research.

Slideshow
View images and captions, and prepare a presentation.

Try This!
Complete activities and hands-on experiments.

... and much, much more!

Published by AV² by Weigl
350 5th Avenue, 59th Floor
New York, NY 10118
Website: www.av2books.com

Library of Congress Control Number: 2018968218

ISBN 978-1-7911-0093-3 (hardcover)
ISBN 978-1-7911-0094-0 (multi-user eBook)
ISBN 978-1-7911-0095-7 (single-user eBook)

Printed in Guangzhou, China
1 2 3 4 5 6 7 8 9 0 23 22 21 20 19

042019
102318

Project Coordinator: Jared Siemens Designer: Terry Paulhus

The publisher acknowledges Alamy, Getty Images, and Wikimedia Commons as its primary image suppliers for this title.

Notre Dame Fighting Irish

CONTENTS

Introduction

The University of Notre Dame was founded in 1842. Nearly 50 years later, the first football team was established. Although it took a few years for the Fighting Irish to start winning, they would eventually become one of the most iconic football teams in the United States.

The Fighting Irish rank fourth in the country for National Championships and boast an impressive seven **Heisman Memorial Trophy** winners. Notre Dame is one of six independent football teams in the National Collegiate Athletic Association (NCAA). This means the Fighting Irish are not part of a conference and can play any teams they choose. All of Notre Dame's home football games have been nationally televised since 1991, which is not true for any other team in the United States.

Defensive lineman Julian Okwara was one of nine true freshman to play in at least eight games during the 2016 season. By 2018, Okwara was an 11-time starter for the Irish.

Notre Dame's classic "Victory March" is one of the most recognizable fight songs in college football. The "Play Like a Champion Today" sign painted above the field entrance has been a part of the team's pregame tradition for four decades. Rich traditions, a strong fan base, and a history of success make the Notre Dame Fighting Irish one of America's favorite college football teams.

Wide receiver Miles Boykin led the Irish during the regular season with 803 receiving yards, and had at least one touchdown catch in six straight games.

NOTRE DAME

Stadium Notre Dame Stadium

Division Independent

Head Coach Brian Kelly

Location Notre Dame, Indiana

National Championships 13

Nicknames The Fighting Irish, The Irish

7 Heisman Trophy Winners

37 Postseason Appearances

112 Seasons Played

52 College Football Hall of Famers

History

Notre Dame is tied with Ohio State University for the most **Heisman Trophy winners.**

When Lou Holtz took over coaching duties at Notre Dame in 1986, he had players' names removed from their jerseys to emphasize team over individuals. Notre Dame players have only worn names on their jerseys six times since then.

The Fighting Irish played their first game in 1887. James Morison was the first head coach. The Knute Rockne era began in 1918. Over his 13 years as coach, Rockne brought Notre Dame onto the national stage with National Championships and winning records. Notre Dame won its first of many National Championships in 1919 and played in its first bowl game in 1925.

The 1940s brought Coach Frank Leahy, a former Notre Dame player, to the team. Leahy led the Fighting Irish to stardom during his 11 seasons as coach. During Leahy's reign, there were many undefeated seasons and a handful of National Championships. Ara Parseghian took over in 1964 and helped coach Notre Dame to two National Championships and two undefeated seasons.

The Irish played in the Cotton Bowl in 1970 and have played in many bowl games since. Head Coach Lou Holtz was hired in 1986, leading the team to yet another national title in 1988. Five coaches and several years later, Brian Kelly was hired in 2010 as Notre Dame's new head coach. The Fighting Irish won the Citrus Bowl in 2017, and fans are hoping their team will continue its upward climb.

In its first five seasons, Notre Dame won 7 of its 11 games, despite not having a coach.

The Stadium

Before the 1997 renovations, Notre Dame Stadium did not have permanent lights. The National Broadcasting Company (NBC) installed the permanent lights for late afternoon games as part of its exclusive television deal with the Fighting Irish.

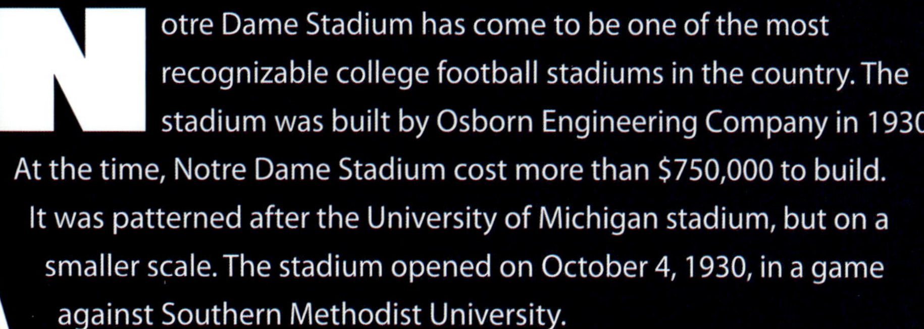

Notre Dame Stadium has come to be one of the most recognizable college football stadiums in the country. The stadium was built by Osborn Engineering Company in 1930. At the time, Notre Dame Stadium cost more than $750,000 to build. It was patterned after the University of Michigan stadium, but on a smaller scale. The stadium opened on October 4, 1930, in a game against Southern Methodist University.

Between 1942 and 1950, the Fighting Irish won 28 straight games in their home stadium. Their ever-supportive fans have helped buoy enthusiasm for the team. These fans have contributed to 268 consecutive sold-out games in Notre Dame Stadium.

Notre Dame Stadium has seen many extensive **renovations**. A $50 million expansion was completed before the 1997 season began. This expansion added 21,000 seats to the stadium. Before the 2009 season, two new scoreboards were installed in both end zones. In 2016, a $400 million renovation added more premium seating, a video board, Wi-Fi, and three new buildings on the stadium's exterior.

The Irish played a game in Yankee Stadium in 2010 and liked the Yankees' video board so much, they decided to get one just like it. The video board, which measures 54 by 96 feet (16 by 29 meters), was installed in 2016.

Where They Play

Welcome to Notre Dame Stadium, home of the Fighting Irish of the University of Notre Dame, where loyal fans have gathered to cheer on the Irish for almost 90 years. The team marches into the stadium surrounded by students and alumni, and the players warm up on the field while the stands fill with gold and blue. The Notre Dame Leprechaun pumps up the crowd, and the marching band plays the Alma Mater. Players and fans sing along to celebrate another Fighting Irish victory in Notre Dame Stadium.

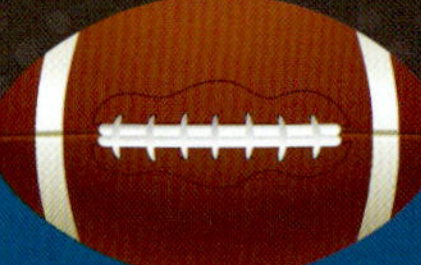

INDEPENDENT

1 **Brigham Young University**
Salt Lake City, Utah

2 **Liberty University**
Lynchburg, Virginia

3 **New Mexico State University**
Las Cruces, New Mexico

4 **United States Military Academy at West Point**
West Point, New York

5 **University of Massachusetts Amherst**
Amherst, Massachusetts

★ 6 **University of Notre Dame**
Notre Dame, Indiana

Arena
Notre Dame Stadium

Location
Notre Dame, Indiana

Broke Ground
1929

Completed
October 4, 1930

Surface
Artifical Turf

Features
- A "Word of Life" mural can be seen from the north end zone
- The 1993 film *Rudy* was partially filmed at the stadium
- A seating capacity of 80,795

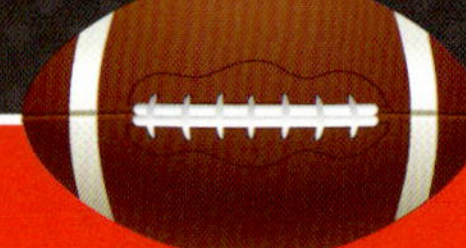

ACC OPPONENTS

In 2014, Notre Dame joined the Atlantic Coast Conference (ACC) in most of the university's sports programs. The football team remains an independent program, but the 24-year agreement with the ACC requires the Fighting Irish to play five ACC opponents in football each season. Notre Dame's ACC opponents are scheduled through 2037. For its remaining seven regular-season games, Notre Dame schedules football games with other schools. The Fighting Irish play the Stanford University Cardinal, the University of Southern California Trojans, and the Navy Midshipmen every season.

MONTANA
NORTH DAKOTA
MINNESOTA
WISCONSIN
MICHIGAN
IDAHO
SOUTH DAKOTA
WYOMING
IOWA
NEW YORK
PENNSYLVANIA
NEW HAMPSHIRE
VERMONT
MAINE
MASSACHUSETTS
RHODE ISLAND
CONNECTICUT
NEW JERSEY
DELAWARE
MARYLAND
WASHINGTON, D.C.
NEBRASKA
ILLINOIS
INDIANA
OHIO
WEST VIRGINIA
VIRGINIA
UTAH
COLORADO
KANSAS
MISSOURI
KENTUCKY
NORTH CAROLINA
TENNESSEE
SOUTH CAROLINA
ARIZONA
NEW MEXICO
OKLAHOMA
ARKANSAS
MISSISSIPPI
ALABAMA
GEORGIA
TEXAS
LOUISIANA
FLORIDA
Atlantic Ocean
Gulf of Mexico
1
2
3
4
5
6
LEGEND
Home Stadium
Independent
United States
Other Countries
Water
SCALE
0 miles
500 miles
0 kilometers
500 km

The Uniforms

The Notre Dame **helmets** used to be spray-painted **gold** before each game with a paint mixture containing **real gold dust**. The gold dust was scraped from the Golden Dome building on campus.

Notre Dame's 2018 Cotton Bowl uniforms were called "Rush 4 Gold" and featured metallic gold accents, including on players' gloves and the bottoms of their Under Armour cleats. The phrase "Rush 4 Gold" was embroidered in gold thread inside the collar.

The very first uniforms worn by the Fighting Irish were all white with a blue "ND" across the chest. Since then, the uniforms have gone through many changes. The 1950s saw the introduction of the team's classic gold helmets. The gold helmets are said to represent the Golden Dome building on campus. They have become a national symbol of the Fighting Irish. In the 1960s, the team briefly had shamrocks on their helmets.

AWAY

Today, the home jerseys are navy blue with white numbers and small interlocking "ND"s on each sleeve. The team wears metallic gold pants and its iconic gold helmets. Each year, Notre Dame plays in a game called the Shamrock Series. Unique uniforms are made for this **annual** tradition. The team uniforms have been made by Under Armour since 2014. Unlike other teams, uniform numbers are not retired at Notre Dame.

The 2015 Shamrock Series uniform featured green jerseys and pants, and Notre Dame's traditional gold helmet. The helmet had a green stripe down the center and the head of the team's traditional leprechaun logo on the side.

Student Athletes

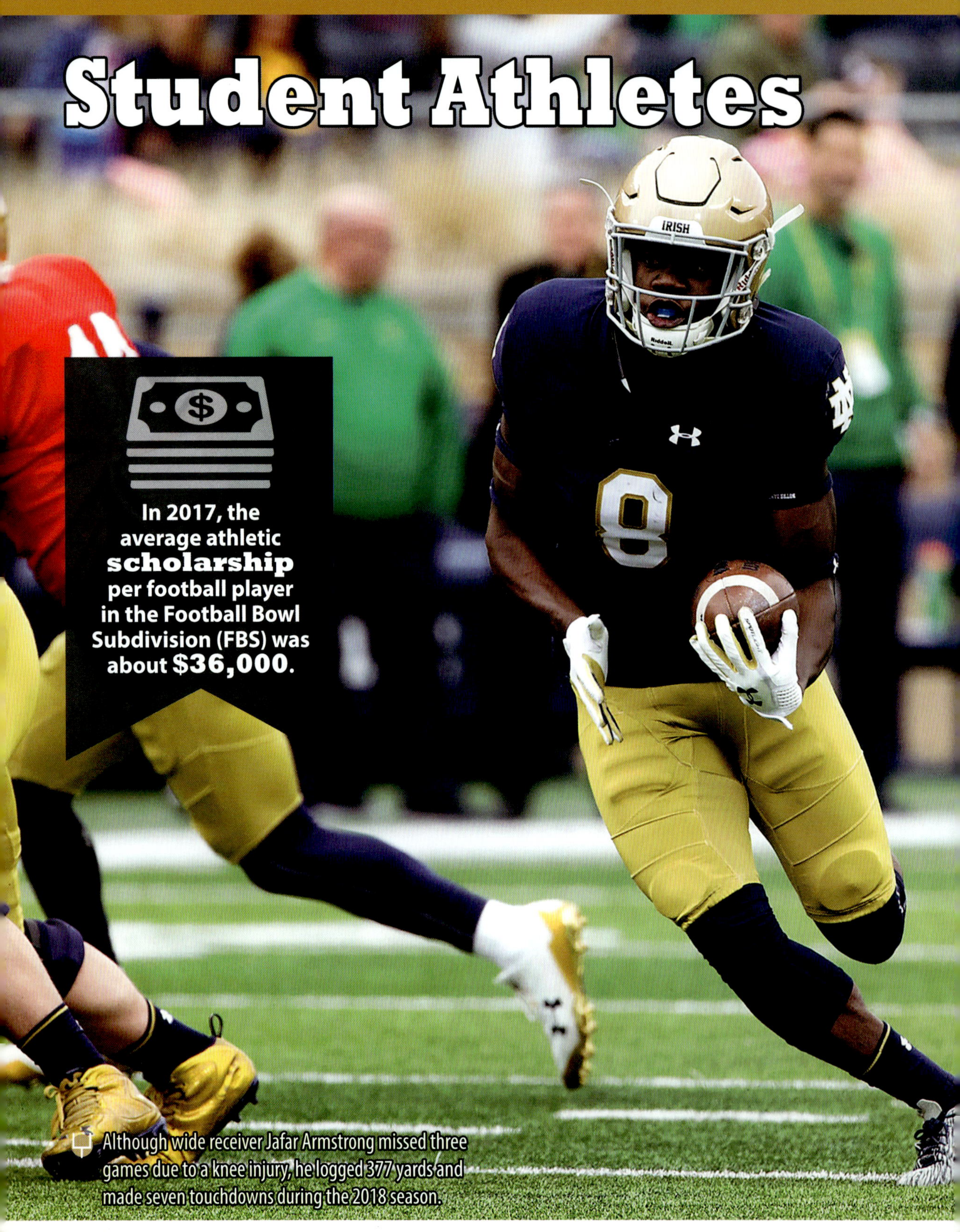

In 2017, the average athletic **scholarship** per football player in the Football Bowl Subdivision (FBS) was about **$36,000**.

Although wide receiver Jafar Armstrong missed three games due to a knee injury, he logged 377 yards and made seven touchdowns during the 2018 season.

Being a college student athlete is hard work. Student athletes have to perform well on the football field and in the classroom. Notre Dame student athletes are required to meet a minimum grade point average and attend all of their classes. They must also have 12 academic credits per term. Athletes at Notre Dame have access to tutoring and time management help. The university offers many other services to help them balance the student athlete life.

Many student athletes are given athletic scholarships. An athletic scholarship is a financial aid agreement between the athlete and the college or university. Athletes who do not receive an athletic scholarship can be "walk-on" members of the team. This means they are on the team but without athletic financial aid. Notre Dame typically awards the maximum number of football scholarships allowed, which is 85.

Defensive lineman Jerry Tillery enrolled at Notre Dame in January of 2015 so he could begin practicing with the team ahead of his freshman season. Tillery graduated in 2018 with an economics degree and finished his football career with multiple team and national honors.

Bowl Games

Notre Dame's **bowl record** is **18–19**.

The Fighting Irish defeated the Louisiana State University Tigers 21–17 in their first Citrus Bowl appearance during the 2017 season.

Bowl games are a unique sports tradition in college football. In the beginning of college football, there was no true postseason. Today, a variety of postseason bowl games are played. Bowl games give teams the opportunity to continue striving for recognition and victory after the end of regular play. There are currently 40 bowl games played in various combinations each year. These games are chosen with input from teams, sponsors, and the College Football Playoff Selection Committee. The game matchups are announced in December.

The Fighting Irish have played in almost 40 bowl games. They have played in many different bowl games, including the Cotton Bowl and the Gator Bowl. Their first bowl game was the Rose Bowl versus Stanford University in 1925. They did not play in another bowl for 45 years. This was because the Notre Dame administration had a "bowl ban," citing academic calendar and travel logistics issues.

Ian Book took over as the Irish's starting quarterback during the 2018 season. He led his team to an undefeated regular season and a spot in the College Football Playoff semifinal versus Clemson University, during which the Tigers defeated Notre Dame 30–3.

The Coaches

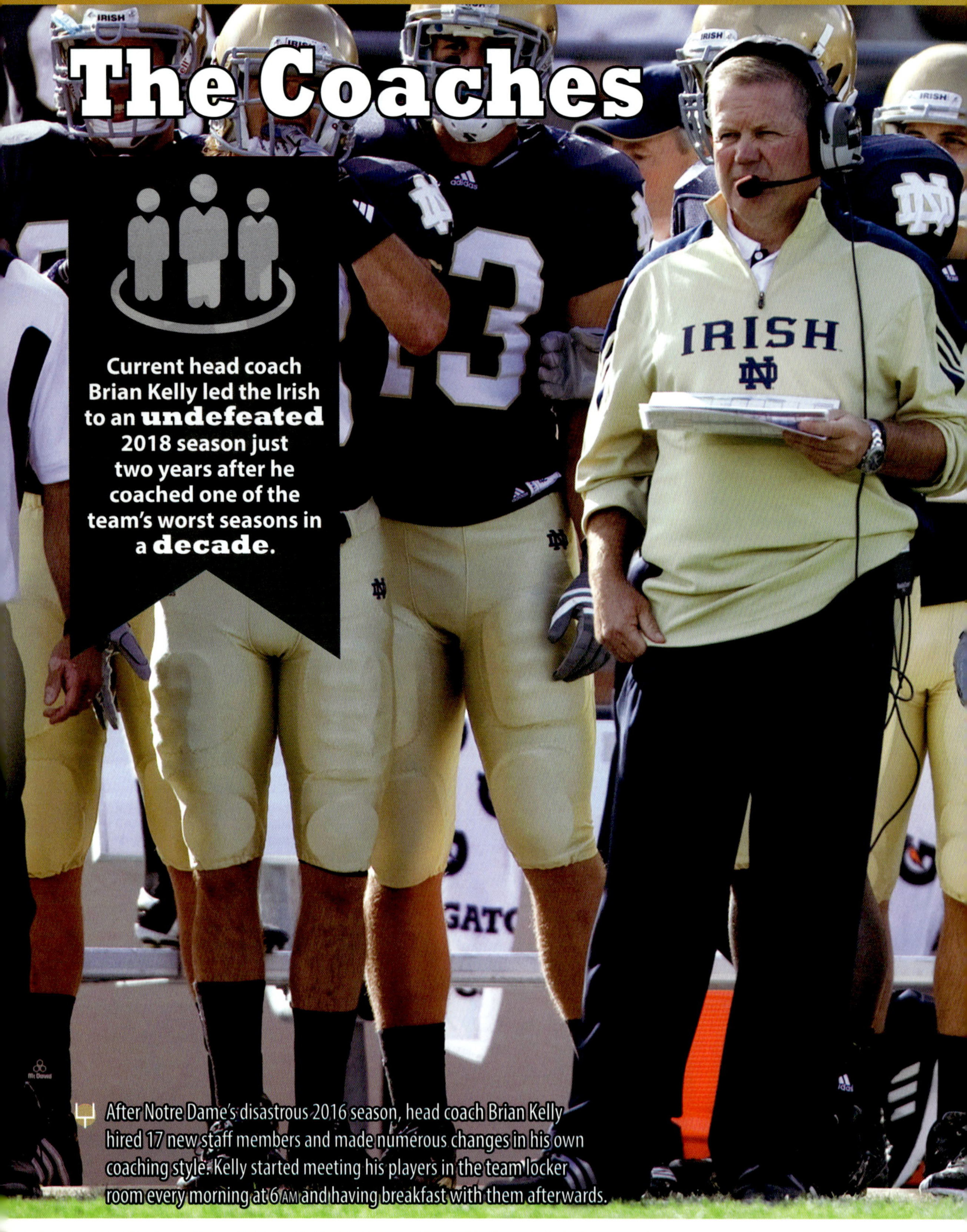

Current head coach Brian Kelly led the Irish to an **undefeated** 2018 season just two years after he coached one of the team's worst seasons in a **decade**.

After Notre Dame's disastrous 2016 season, head coach Brian Kelly hired 17 new staff members and made numerous changes in his own coaching style. Kelly started meeting his players in the team locker room every morning at 6 AM and having breakfast with them afterwards.

Notre Dame has been coached by some of college football's most well-known coaches. Knute Rockne is considered the face of college football. He coached notable players such as George Gipp and the "Four Horsemen of Notre Dame," the famous backfield from his 1924 team. Frank Leahy became head coach in 1941 and led the Fighting Irish to six undefeated seasons. Ara Parseghian helped restore Notre Dame to football glory when he took over in the 1960s.

KNUTE ROCKNE Rockne played football at Notre Dame himself before becoming the head coach and athletic director in 1918. He coached until 1930 and built Notre Dame into a national powerhouse during his 13 seasons with the team. The Fighting Irish had five undefeated seasons and won three National Championships under Rockne's leadership.

FRANK LEAHY Leahy took the helm in the early 1940s and led Notre Dame to a record-setting unbeaten streak of 39 consecutive games from 1946 to 1950. Under Leahy's leadership, the team won four National Championships with an overall record of 87–11–9. Leahy had a .855 winning percentage, the third-highest in Notre Dame history. He retired from coaching in 1953.

ARA PARSEGHIAN Parseghian's first year as Notre Dame's head coach was 1964. He is best known for helping turn around the struggling football program, securing national titles in both 1966 and 1973. He coached 21 consensus **All-Americans** with a .836 winning percentage. His record in 11 years of coaching was 95–17–4. Parseghian retired from coaching after the 1974 season and became a sports broadcaster.

The Mascot

Although leprechauns in Irish mythology are hard to find, the Notre Dame Leprechaun is an enthusiastic, outspoken symbol of the university's Irish history and winning spirit.

The mascot for the Fighting Irish is a costumed leprechaun. The Leprechaun was designed by artist Theodore W. Drake and became the school's official mascot in 1965. He wears a green suit and an Irish hat. He also carries a *shillelagh*, which is a stick associated with Irish folklore. He is thought to bring good luck to the school.

The Leprechaun is the master of ceremonies, or MC, at the university's Friday night pep rallies. He performs Irish jigs and leads the cheers in the student section at games. The student section is called Leprechaun Legion. The Leprechaun is quite famous, and even appeared on the cover of *Time* magazine in 1964. In 2013, the university **unveiled** a statue of the mascot on its campus.

Students who audition to be the official Notre Dame Leprechaun must attend a week-long training session and participate in formal interviews with university administration, coaches, and members of the Notre Dame Alumni Association.

Legends of the Past

For many players, their time with the Fighting Irish is the start of a promising football career. These are some of the best-known football players to play for Notre Dame.

Joe Montana

Joe Montana, affectionately known as "Joe Cool," is quite possibly the most famous quarterback of all time. During his time at Notre Dame, Montana had 25 touchdowns and 4,121 passing yards. He also helped lead the Irish to their 1977 national title. Montana went on to have a very successful National Football League (NFL) career, playing for 15 years and winning four Super Bowls. He played with the San Francisco 49ers for 13 seasons, before playing for the Kansas City Chiefs for 2 seasons. Montana was inducted into the Pro Football **Hall of Fame** in 2000.

Position: Quarterback
Seasons: 1974–1978 (Notre Dame Fighting Irish), 1979–1992 (San Francisco 49ers), 1993–1994 (Kansas City Chiefs)
Born: June 11, 1956, New Eagle, Pennsylvania

George Gipp

George Gipp is a Notre Dame **legend**. Gipp began playing at Notre Dame in 1917. Playing under Coach Rockne, he was Notre Dame's first All-American. Gipp played in 32 straight games and made 83 touchdowns. In 1920, his senior year, Gipp helped lead the Irish to a 9–0 season. During a 1928 game with the U.S. Military Academy Army Cadets, Coach Rockne told the team to "win one for the Gipper." Notre Dame went on to beat the Army Cadets, fulfilling a promise Rockne had made to Gipp, who passed away in 1920 of an illness. The phrase "win one for the Gipper" became a well-known rallying cry for the Irish.

Position: Running Back
Seasons: 1917–1920 (Notre Dame Fighting Irish)
Born: February 18, 1895, Laurium, Michigan

Harrison Smith

Harrison Smith began his football career at Notre Dame as a linebacker, but eventually ended up as safety. Smith was team captain during the 2011 season, his final year at Notre Dame, and was the only Fighting Irish player to have more than 200 tackles. He was a first-round NFL **draft** pick with the Minnesota Vikings in 2012. Smith signed a five-year contract extension in 2016, making him one of the NFL's highest-paid safeties. Smith was named an **All-Pro** first team in 2017.

Position: Safety
Seasons: 2007–2011 (Notre Dame Fighting Irish), 2012–Present (Minnesota Vikings)
Born: February 2, 1989, Augusta, Georgia

Zack Martin

Zack Martin helped Notre Dame achieve a 12–0 regular-season record in 2012. He was one of the Fighting Irish's team captains and led them on their National Championship run that same year. Martin was also named **Most Valuable Player (MVP)** of the Pinstripe Bowl in 2013. He went on to become a first-round draft pick for the Dallas Cowboys in 2014. He has been named to the All-Pro first team every year he has played in the NFL. In 2018, Martin signed a six-year contract extension with the Cowboys, making him the highest-paid guard in the NFL.

Position: Offensive Guard
Seasons: 2009–2013 (Notre Dame Fighting Irish), 2014–Present (Dallas Cowboys)
Born: November 20, 1990, Indianapolis, Indiana

All-Time Records

6
Single-Game Touchdown Passes
Brady Quinn broke the school record during a 2005 game against Brigham Young University, with six passing touchdowns.

367
Points Scored
Justin Yoon is Notre Dame's top scorer of all time. Yoon scored 367 points from 2015 to 2018 as the Irish's kicker.

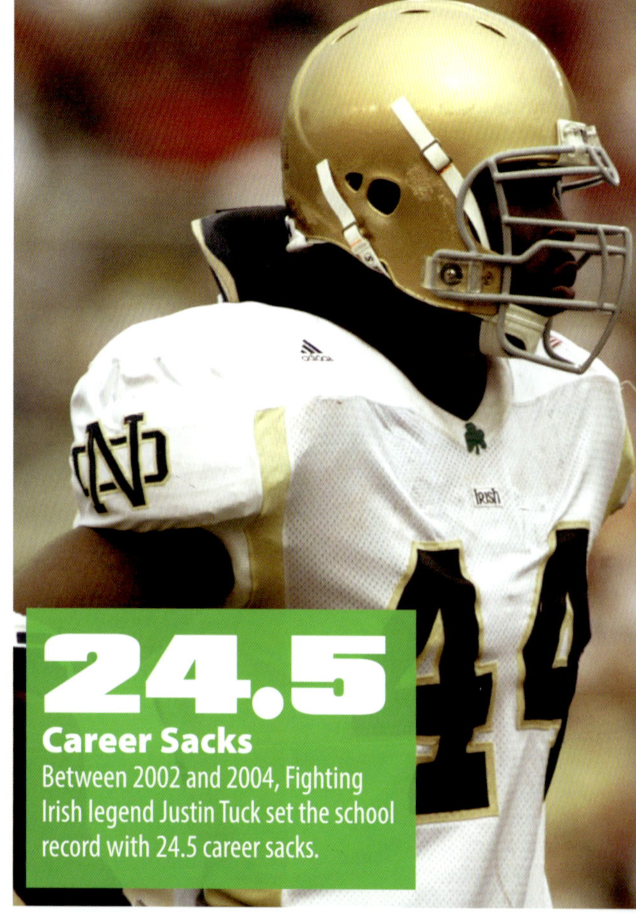

24.5
Career Sacks
Between 2002 and 2004, Fighting Irish legend Justin Tuck set the school record with 24.5 career sacks.

526

Single-Game Passing Yards

Quarterback Joe Theismann had 526 passing yards in a 1970 game, breaking the school record for passing yards. His record still stands today.

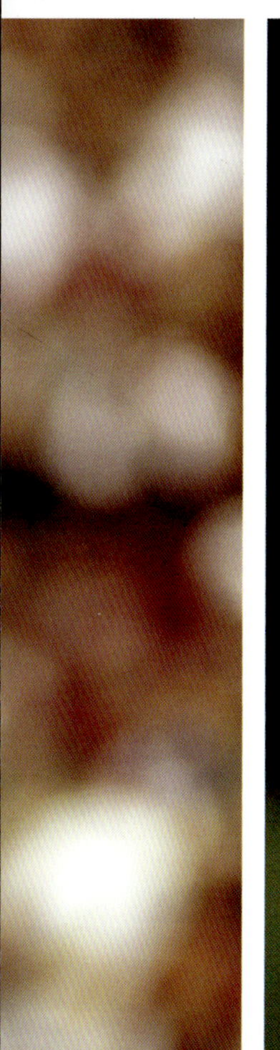

101

Most Career Touchdowns

Brady Quinn holds the Fighting Irish record for most career touchdowns, with 101 from 2003 to 2006.

Timeline

Throughout the team's history, the Notre Dame Fighting Irish have had many memorable events that have become defining moments for the team and its fans.

1887
Notre Dame plays its first game against the University of Michigan.

1964
Ara Parseghian is hired to take over as head coach and launches the team into a decade of winning seasons.

1900 1920 1940 1960

In 1919, the Fighting Irish win their first National Championship.

1930
Notre Dame Stadium is built at the urging of Coach Rockne, and is completed a few months before Rockne is killed in a plane crash.

1988
The Irish are undefeated and win the National Championship.

1970
The Irish play in the Cotton Bowl, their first bowl game after the 45-year "bowl ban."

The Future
The Irish are one of college football's winningest teams and continue to produce Hall of Famers, All-Americans, and NFL standouts. With a perfect finish going into the 2018 postseason, Notre Dame is hoping for another golden era of football. With veteran defensive players and an outstanding quarterback, Brian Kelly's Irish have a shot at another National Championship.

The Irish are undefeated in the 2018 season and win a spot in the Cotton Bowl, one of the semifinal games of the College Football Playoffs.

1980 2000 2020

2012
Coach Kelly and the Irish end the 2012 season undefeated for the first time since 1993, but lose the National Championship 42–14 to the University of Alabama Crimson Tide. Due to NCAA sanctions, the Irish are forced to vacate their 11 wins from 2012.

Write a Biography

Life Story

A person's life story can be the subject of a book. This kind of book is called a biography. Biographies often describe the lives of people who have achieved great success. These people may be alive today, or they may have lived many years ago. Reading a biography can help you learn more about a great person.

Get the Facts

Use this book, and research in the library and on the internet, to find out more about your favorite player. Learn as much about him as you can. What position does he play? What are his statistics in important categories? Has he set any records? Also, be sure to write down key events in the person's life. What was his childhood like? What has he accomplished off the field? Is there anything else that makes this person special or unusual?

Use the Concept Web

A concept web is a useful research tool. Read the questions in the concept web on the following page. Answer the questions in your notebook. Your answers will help you write a biography.

Concept Web

Your Opinion
- What did you learn from the books you read in your research?
- Would you suggest these books to others?
- Was anything missing from these books?

Adulthood
- Where does this individual currently reside?
- Does he have a family?

Childhood
- Where and when was this person born?
- Describe his parents, siblings, and friends.
- Did he grow up in unusual circumstances?

Accomplishments off the Field
- What is this person's life's work?
- Has he received awards or recognition for accomplishments?
- How have this person's accomplishments served others?

Write a Biography

Help and Obstacles
- Did this individual have a positive attitude?
- Did he receive help from others?
- Did this person have a mentor?
- Did this person face any hardships?
- If so, how were the hardships overcome?

Accomplishments on the Field
- What records does this person hold?
- What key games and plays have defined his career?
- What are his stats in categories important to his position?

Work and Preparation
- What was this person's education?
- What was his work experience?
- How does this person work?
- What is the process he uses?

Trivia Time

Take this quiz to test your knowledge of the Notre Dame Fighting Irish. The answers are printed upside down under each question.

1 All of Notre Dame's home games have been nationally televised since what year?

A. 1991

2 How many consecutive sold-out games have been played in Notre Dame Stadium?

A. 268

3 How many football scholarships does the NCAA allow per team each season?

A. 85

4 What are Notre Dame's gold helmets said to represent?

A. The Golden Dome building on campus

5 What is Notre Dame's mascot?

A. A leprechaun

6 How many national championships has Notre Dame won?

A. 13

7 In which year did Notre Dame play its first season of football?

A. 1887

8 Which skilled Notre Dame quarterback went on to win four Super Bowls in the NFL?

A. Joe Montana

9 How many years did Notre Dame's "bowl ban" last?

A. 45

10 Which former Notre Dame player led the team to 87 total victories as head coach?

A. Frank Leahy

Key Words

All-Americans: players, usually in high school or college, judged to be the best in each position of a sport

All-Pro: a term used to designate the best players of each position during a given season

annual: something that occurs once a year

draft: an annual event where the NFL chooses college football players to be new team members

Hall of Fame: a group of persons judged to be outstanding in a particular sport

Heisman Memorial Trophy: an annual award given to the college football player who best demonstrates excellence and hard work

legend: an extremely well-known or famous person

Most Valuable Player (MVP): the player judged to be most valuable to his team's success

renovations: construction that works to improve or expand an older building

unveiled: to show something in public for the first time

Index

Log on to www.av2books.com

AV² by Weigl brings you media enhanced books that support active learning. Go to www.av2books.com, and enter the special code found on page 2 of this book. You will gain access to enriched and enhanced content that supplements and complements this book. Content includes video, audio, weblinks, quizzes, a slideshow, and activities.

AV² Online Navigation

Audio
Listen to sections of the book read aloud.

Book Pages
AV² pages directly correspond to pages in the book.

Video
Watch informative video clips.

Embedded Weblinks
Gain additional information for research.

Key Words
Study vocabulary, and complete a matching word activity.

Try This!
Complete activities and hands-on experiments.

Quizzes
Test your knowledge.

Slideshow
View images and captions, and prepare a presentation.

AV² was built to bridge the gap between print and digital. We encourage you to tell us what you like and what you want to see in the future.

Sign up to be an AV² Ambassador at www.av2books.com/ambassador.

Due to the dynamic nature of the internet, some of the URLs and activities provided as part of AV² by Weigl may have changed or ceased to exist. AV² by Weigl accepts no responsibility for any such changes. All media enhanced books are regularly monitored to update addresses and sites in a timely manner. Contact AV² by Weigl at 1-866-649-3445 or av2books@weigl.com with any questions, comments, or feedback.